Bloom

Decima Wraxall has won prizes for essays. Her short stories and poems have appeared in various journals. A humorous article appeared in the *Australian Women's Weekly*. Her novel *Black Stockings, White Veil, a Tale of Adversity, Triumph and Romance at Royal Prince Alfred Hospital* was a finalist in the 2009 Next Generation Indie Book Awards for Historical Fiction. Continuing the historical theme, her book *Letters From a Digger, a Tale of Loyalty and Courage In World War I* was published in 2015. Her next book in the duo, *Going Home*, is having final edits. Decima has co-edited two anthologies – *Our Women's Work* and *Bare*, both from the Women Writer's Network at the NSW Writers' Centre. The former anthology was a finalist in the 2014 Next Generation Indie Book Awards for Women's Issues. In 2017 Decima won a place at Varuna Writers' House for a week's focus on poetry with Vanessa Kirkpatrick.

Decima Wraxall

Bloom

Bloom
ISBN 978 1 76041 696 6
Copyright © text Decima Wraxall 2019
Copyright © cover painting Melissa Wraxall 2018

First published 2019 by
Ginninderra Press
PO Box 3461 Port Adelaide 5015
www.ginninderrapress.com.au

Contents

Lower the Flags	9
Bluff	11
Glass Eye	12
Living Fossils	14
Hands	15
Worry Beads	19
Doppelganger	21
Gourmet Beef Pie	22
Black Dog	23
Singles Night	24
MONA	25
Death Row	27
Glitter	29
Daisy Cooper	30
Kiss	31
Refugees	32
Katoomba Heist	33
Talk to Yourself	34
Bliss	36
Gowns at an Exhibition	37
Dubai Guest Worker	38
King's Canyon, NT	39
Inner Walls	40
Gold	41
private	42
Snowy Mountains	43
Orbs of Wonder	44
Icarus Moment	45
Molly	47
The Three Sisters	49
Mute	50

Clearing	52
Pompom Parade	53
Chainsaw Hero	54
Trophy	55
No Cause No Reason	56
Farewell Visit	57
Incan Idyll	59
Squirrel Maths	61
Psychiatry Ward	62
Massacre	64
Incongruous	65
Celebration of Day	66
Fox	67
Uluru Caper	68
Don't Call Me Madam	70
Prickle Bush	71
Naked	73
Parched	74
Perfection	76
Time for Lunch	77
Master Two	78
Paradox	79
Mellow Sunday	80
Pisco Sour	81
Cambridge Man	83
Paean	84
Cairns Rendezvous	85
Indian Hawker	86
Gallipoli	87
Sacred Moments	88
Bachelors' Buttons	89
Caijon Del Maipo	91
Rains of Change	93

Perfect Evening	94
Eternal Land	95
Boneyard	96
Breathless	97
Emotions	98
Greetings	99
Fig Tart and Tea	102
Earthquake	103
Dad	104
Epiphany	105
A Grief Ago	106
Ella	107
Abu Dhabi	108
Gone	109
Hovercraft XPT	110
Goodbye	112
Frozen Time	114
Greek Tragedy	115
Hatzolah	116
Slippery Trout	117
Last Trip to Manly	118
Waiting for a Train	120
Malingering	121
Mall Dreaming	122
Sacred Rites	123
Sardonic	125
Athens Train	126
Gather	127
Rescue	128
Dazzle	129
Fallen Star	130

Lower the Flags

Beach glitter, placid sea
red and yellow flutter.
Tide turns, scud of clouds

Gusty winds, roiling surf.
Rips flare, splash, crash, roar.
Lifesavers scramble.

Tom helps: a dozen rescues.
Two victims pale, motionless.
Plangent wail, each ambulance

scintillates, red and blue.

His last patient. She's
ashen, eyes rolled back,
weak pulse. Compression,

oxygen, ECG. He fears brain
damage. Help screams her away.
He stores red and yellow flags.

Numb disbelief, long debrief.
It happened so fast…
He longs to see her.

Paramedics warn, don't
go, mate, more trauma.
Days later she visits.

His goosebumps rush into
gratitude – longest hug of his life.
She laughs. *Want to thank you,*

for saving me.
But, gosh, my sore ribs.

Bluff

Tall, patched trousers, hobnailed boots.
Bushman's friendly grin. Dad saying, *You'll have
to excuse me, chaps, if I can't keep up.
Hip replacements, dicky ticker.*
His doctor's warning, *Stick to flat ground,*
not even a thought,
on his horizon.

Energy and youth led the way. But soon
Dad strode on past. City chaps slipping and sliding
up that vertiginous bluff. Dad's mountain legs
kept on striding. At the top, he stopped,
haunches on a rock.
Surprised to see those younger men
puffing, breathless, trailing far behind.

Dad doffed his sweat-stained hat to the flies. And, eyes
closed, he rested, dappled by kurrajong shade.
The others made it to his side, perspiring, faces aflame.
One gasped, *Bad heart? Hip replacements?
I'd give a thousand quid,*

for your surgeon to see you now.

Glass Eye

At first glance, an eye like yours and mine.
One of many John wears – growing up.
Designed with sensitivity to anatomy

and artistic skill. It's blue-grey, flecks
and veins in place. And he can't see
well enough with the other eye,

to read signs or timetables.
His glass replica – not the sort
of thing one chooses

to hold in the hand.
Yet it was his dad's hand
that stole most of John's sight –

balled into a fist. Many times
he's beaten until the blood runs –
the boy keeps his gob shut.

Youngest child, only son, seven sisters.
I hear them crying at night – guess
what me dad had done.

Hate him, love my mum.
At sixteen he learns to box,
tells no one. *Next time the old man*

clenches his fists, I throw
him into the dam. Hope
he'll drown, but mum

shouts, Don't kill him, son –
who'll feed me?
John drags him out, coughing

and spluttering, eyes bulging.
He's shaking like a fish.
John stares him down.

Never again touch
me sisters or me mum,
or that'll be the last time

anyone sees you alive.
John strokes his glass eye.

Living Fossils

in shallow pools   heavy
with saline   lulled by the rush
and shush of distant waves
round rocks laze and sunbathe

layered mounds   formed
from accretion of solid parts
stromatolites   cyanobacteria
billions per square metre

do they ask if it was God
who sent them to seed the earth?
or a chance gift
from space?

in the long glitter of summer days
do they discuss their aerobic importance?
Darwin's concept of evolution?

new bacteria bask in the light
copious photosynthesisers
growing a fraction of a millimetre
each year

do they boast to the young
how three billion years ago
their ancestors

shaped the environment?
with oxygen
for life on earth?

Hands

for Joe

i

Your hands were huge and square, palms
calloused, from axe, saw, pick and shovel.
Age and arthritis leaving some fingers bent
south, others worn and crippled.

As a child their mottled skin didn't matter,
until one woman's idle chatter, saying,
Ugh! What horrible hands,

bringing shame without a name.
You carried your burden seventy years or more,
hefting strainer posts, calming babies, making love.
Until a starched nurse caressed them on the quilt,
voice soft as silk, Oh! What lovely hands!

A lifetime's guilt smoothed away,
by her grace and caring words.
Doctors and physios gazed,
at their size, amazed.

A sculptor cast one in bronze –
their final absolution.

ii

Your hands gathered hard white spuds,
unearthed, by tractor and plough.
It was bend, gather, throw.
Gather and stand, throw.

For you to bag and sew later.
Row after row, bend, gather, throw.
Elongated shadows, grotesque
distortions, in rainbows of dew.

The brazen sun slips low, lower.
Golden light bathes eucalypts,
on the hill. Aching, fading still.
Until twilight drinks the last

colour from the day. Now it's grey,
turning black. Bend, gather, throw,
stand, walk, gather… In the gloom,
you grapple for another spud.

Your weary hand grabs
instead a funnel web.
Its ferocious fangs no match,
for your leathered palm.

iii

Tomalla Creek runs away for the sea.
Your questing hands, seek an Eldorado,
of hopes and dreams. On your haunches
boots wet, stream chatter, bird twitter.

Fingers heft the metal dish, brimful
with soil and water, inside an indented
ring. You shake the dish, dip, swirl. Pour
cloudy water, flowing now the fresh.

Your big fingers brush aside gravel,
tease away the last grains of sand.
The dish light and nigh empty.
Except for glitter, a pennyweight
of gold.

iv

If you were here now,
I'd ask you to tell me again,
what it was like,
during the Great Depression.

When bush work petered out.
And you felt lucky
to have rabbit stew, on the menu.
And the one hope, for survival,

of an itinerant man like you,
to garner gold from the creek,
with eager hands. And now
your penetrating glance,

shimmers before me,
in the mellow afternoon light.
I'm surprised, to see you there,
years after slipping away.

As if, even now, you mean
to set off in hobnailed boots
and patched trousers.

Mining dish in hand…

Worry Beads

i gaze at athens' remnant glories   ancient monuments
and broken columns aroma of *kouloria* crisp bread circles
with sesame seeds   shiver in the icy breeze   bar lights
blink white   green and red *zorbas* smoke cough and toss
worry beads   sipping tiny cups of black coffee   four
hundred drachmas – aroma free   the barista hands me
change for five hundred   my jet-lagged head spins   hadn't
i given a thousand? he loses his english…

potholes leer and paint peels   in omonia square
an elderly greek   olive-smooth of cheek   waxed
moustache twitching   offers to show me around
i make my escape   panepistimiou street
stretches in the sun   ritzy clothing and 18-carat gold
ready to caress and possess   black-clad granny
begging bowl and crutches   sits in the dust
her note   *spare a few drachmas*

perfumed roses and orchids   look the other way
hiding behind a riot of colours   *peripetero* man
brings postcards   souvenirs   trinkets – and rainbows
of dreams – chance numbers   allure of haunting
oriental music   long raven hair   carmine roses
and voluptuous eyes promise delights
of boudoir and cuisine

teenage girl   hopeless air   scrofulous hound on rope
scrawled   *no home no job – please help*   beasts
of athens roar   brakes screech   sirens wail
swapped car days curse   barely moving
motorbikes short-cut pavements
white-gloved cop's whistle shrieks
pedestrians zigzag across street
traffic rage chokes on fumes
coach miscalculates   backs up
female driver leaps and screams
take a different line –
or my car will be crushed

mid-morning   crumbling monuments
gag on pungent air   risk asphyxiation
metro promised soon…

Doppeganger

it was uncanny to see
the little blonde girl
on a river ferry   double
of me at two or three

child of the forties in
the twenty-first century
how could that be? Same
chubby legs and shy smile

her eyes so like mine
seen in a mirror long ago
at home   i studied
a black and white photo

taken back then
was my memory playing
tricks? but no: it could be
her standing there beside

my brother   gazing at kittens

Gourmet Beef Pie

in the mellow light
candles dance betrayal
he longs to slip inside

his gourmet beef pie
hidden by truffle sauce
until his secret lover

fades away
he turns to his darling
grin wide as sin

more champagne my lovely?
he leans closer   whispers
i've just spotted a lady

i once knew
mad   poor thing
harmless enough

bound to say hello
on passing our table
let me handle this

don't say a word
or glance her way
lest things escalate

into a scene
he blushes like a boy

what the hell might she say?

Black Dog

The hound howled
through classical mythology
growled in mediaeval folklore
opaque canine of despair.
Victims of this hellhound

can't eat, can't sleep.
Thoughts elusive, confidence
eroded, anxiety a given, dragged
down by interminable time.
Craving only the relief of sleep.

Horace, Roman lyric poet
wrote of melancholy
the fight to live, the wish to die.
And, century after century
this beast, shade of the devil,

has claimed its prey.
You can't snap out of it:
only time, therapy or pills heal.
Apollonius of Tyana, orator
and philosopher, spoke of
this witches familiar, guarding

the world of the dead.
Winston Churchill cited,
endured and transcended
this relentless companion.
And, after long, dark days

of World War Two,
he introduced his black dog
to the world.

Singles Night

blondie's frenzied mating dance   alone
layered paint   crow's feet smile
bling   baubles bounce

cleavage wobbles   stiletto leaps
skirt around her thighs
impress the punters

blokes   baggage   beer guts
burp   *what's yer name again?*
matey smoke signals of deceit

only came for the feed
one question in their eyes
does she?

and blondie bowls over
a potted palm

MONA

in the sparkle of hobart town
this gamblers dream – a museum
hewn from sandstone – is built to give

the impression of a single-storey building
it burrows deep into the earth   becoming
a poem in glass and stone   the see-through
elevator speeds us to levels far below

exhibitions of erotica   may confront
one woman spends five hours
in contemplation and wants more

another walks out   after twenty minutes
disgusted   over female genitalia
transformed into flower sculptures

and male bits   well hung   presented
as art   touch-pad phones bring info   antique
chairs stare at mellow sandstone walls   drawings

of red riding hood   leave the hungry wolf   too close
and poetic exploration of love in its myriad dimensions
provoke anxiety   in the mother of an adult daughter –

some mildly risqué stanza – her *sotto voce*: *don't read
it aloud dear*   had me stifling giggles   i climbed
the ladder   sensible to the sweet music

of revelation   wrought to body and soul
each poem exulting in the mystery
and magic of human relations

and the theme of approaching death
echoed from the shine of egyptian
artefacts   rescued from oblivion's grasp
mona stars in landscaped gardens
among cycads   the most ancient
plants on earth with vistas of vineyards
trees   rolling hills and harbour

Death Row

i

Can't eat can't sleep. i dread another walk down that corridor of death. Chaotic childhood. Nobody cared. Small crime conviction. Innocent, found guilty. Angry, wanted to get even. Lied to myself, lied to others. Now my sister visits twice weekly. She makes me feel human. In the aroma of coffee, I gaze at the moon and stars, striped by bars. Morning sparrows twitter, pecking crumbs from the sill. Free to fly… I've learnt to read and write. Keep myself in the present, moment by moment.

ii

Nun, spiritual advisor, friend. She holds my hands, brings peace – even hope. It's a surreal journey – so many appeals stopped at the brink. Jumpy as a flea, I seek redemption. She's taught me how to love. It's a beautiful feeling.

iii

I took a father's only son. The old man said, *Boy and man, he was loving and kind. – someone killed my son – but he won't kill me.* His anguished face haunts my dreams Apology, forgiveness – but how can I forgive myself? I burn with shame and regret. This man's courage amazes me. He says, *must have been his time*.

iv

Vengeance awaits my execution – read his letter in the paper. Guards with rifles will hover, scared I'll try a runner. Strap-down team, incontinence pad. I hope the lethal injection works quickly. Sometimes death waits, reluctant… Vengeance will carry one regret.

SOB died too fast

Glitter

morning glitter
dances on my wardrobe knob
seven last words
of Christ on the Cross
from my radio

Daisy Cooper

daisy's face lights up   *oh goody*   *you're here*
feisty   great smile
radio plays macca and bird calls
daisy stretches gaunt legs
to keep fit
i dress the boil on her bottom
she hits her head
glancing blow   big bruise
daisy laughs   *now I've problems*
at both ends

tremor in her voice
raped at twenty
now I'm ninety
physio tried to make me
walk the corridor three times
she says age just a state of mind
told her go fly a kite
not doing it   and that's that

that sunday should've guessed
daisy short of breath frail
don't be angry, sister
had a little turn
asked the lord to take me
as you can see   he didn't

dear daisy
feel gutted   left late
didn't get to say goodbye

Kiss

cherry tree   veiled in white
pollen   for the bees
stolen kiss   and laughter
trembling   on the breeze

Refugees

concorde replicas in flight
long legs folded   in their wake
        curved stilettos thrust forward
ibis leave parched wetlands

to find board and lodging
in Sydney streets
        high in the ramparts   of urban peaks
they mock dinner chimes
of the central clock

below a bus groans at red delay
flash of green as it drives away

beggar solicits coins
haunted   eyes watching an ibis dive
into the gutter   fighting off pigeons

for a dried-out crust

Katoomba Heist

Someone's nicked an icon
the three sisters, leaving only
their cloaks in white –

draped over the valley
Was it a heist at midnight?
Thieves intent on gaining

their prize – however big
or small the size?
Perhaps they plan to ship them

overseas, guarded by DC3s?
Someone should warn
the cops – before crims try

to fence 'em in the shops.

Talk to Yourself

nobody doubts your statements
then asks you to repeat   or says can you
count backwards in threes?

nobody cries *speak louder*
or puts you down
and tells you *say that again*

nobody says *how long
since they've checked
your hearing aids?*

nobody says *you told me that already*
and fires a fusillade of questions
you don't care to answer

it's easy to feel more intelligent
when you talk to yourself –
too bad some think you're mad

Luscious

A fig tree grows beside the burbling brook of childhood
loaded with luscious fruit. I munch from sun-warmed skin
to the soft interior, my mouth exults in every squishy bite.
Drooling at taste sensations dating to biblical times. The lobed
palmate leaves of light green were used, Holy Scripture says,
to sew garments hiding naked Eve and the fallen Adam –
my treasure nestles between those special leaves.
I sway on slender branches beneath the radiant sky.
My hands drip fragrant juice, I salivate plucking one
delight after another, until mum asserts I've had enough.
Now, I garner this taste sensation from supermarket shelves –
priced like gold. I recall the sensual pleasure of youthful feasts,
delay the moment, savour the smell, anticipate the taste, and eye
the purple, striated skin, fruit rounded and green towards the stem.
At last, biting through soft flesh, multiple tiny seeds, edible and pinkish,
caress my tongue. Sapor explodes in my mouth. Eve knew a thing or two.

Bliss

the labrador places one black paw
after another with precaution
eyes and ears swivel

alert to every danger
ready to disobey
to save his walker's life

soon to join his new owner
she's blind   he'll curb his hunger
and sit still   until her shrill whistle

marks his time to eat
unexpected reunion
the smell   the touch

of his first foster family
paroxysms of joy
who to welcome first?

he rushes between their legs
leaps   licks and yips
first one   then the other

groans at their caress
and bliss quivers
from nose to tail

Gowns at an Exhibition

Midnight-blue lace, spangled
with stars. Twilight sonata corset
for a courtesan. Golden glow shine.

Feather stitch, whip stitch, French knots.

Rose-pink silk, jewelled bodice
moulded on the reef. Skirt trails
tendrils, sparkle, shimmy of fragile life.

Hand-painting, Angelina fibres, Mossing.

Golden phoenix glitter, merchant treasure.
Gilded carnival masks, Vivaldi masquerade.
Ball bubble skirt, antique lace, powdered gold.

Embroidered silk, *nuno* felt, appliqué.

Rendezvous, Pont deVecchio. Smooth shoulders
jewelled throat. Gossamer silk organza flutter
glimpses of love, stroked by an angel's wing.

Three needle thread, bling, beads and braiding.

Sew your poem of textiles, vistas of the mind
and human endeavour. Spirit of Balenciaga
Yves St Laurent and Coco Chanel.

Escape your chrysalis
become the sublime

Dubai Guest Worker

chill afternoon   far from his homeland he drives a four by four –
   adventure
tours working late each evening

meagre wage   dunes sighing of exile   engine roar unbalanced
   wobble
tilting dive   wheels spinning   flaccid

tyres barely gaining traction   vanquish sandy walls   somehow
   he keeps the
vehicle from overturning   thump bump

under a veiled red sun   tourists
   scream laugh giggle   softly night steals
beneath the desert stars

rich aromas   grilled steaks sausages
   and incense   bells bling belly dancer
mirrors men's undulating eyes   henna

designs on western hands   dinner over camel handlers heading
   home   the driver pumps up the tyres
drops his guests at five-star hotels

he caresses the mobile phone
   aglow at his wife's voice   two months home every summer
daughter he barely knows

King's Canyon, NT

admire the garden of eden   at king's canyon
sacred to aborigines   they never dared mark
its walls with rock paintings

we swim and play
in lush waterholes   ignorant of spiritual
connections   but impressions show

waves from long-ago beaches
solidified in sandstone
it's four hundred thousand years

since dinosaurs swam here
and cycads grew in the rainforest
man brought dreamtime rituals

and ceremonies   these ancient
palms live on in desert oases
treasured in city gardens

Inner Walls

fear of the other
and simplistic solutions
to complex questions

build inner walls
seek truth and reason
break down barriers

between creeds and cultures
let's discover how they see us
it's easy to denigrate the sightless

other   ignoring our own blindfolds
and say all would be felicity
if they went away

irrational opinions bring
despair   precluding others
from growth decency and love

let's have the grace to embrace
complexity   engender humanity
and find the common thread

that binds us as one

Gold

i love the burnished gold windows
greeting me at rose cottage
on summer afternoons

mother has coaxed blossoms
from neglected roses
in the abandoned garden

they speak to me
in the language of flowers
red fragrance   velvet voice

the mock orange clad in white
kissed by bees
whispers its heady scent

trixie runs to meet me
black and white purrs of delight
her fur caresses my bare legs

i munch an apple
crisp from the orchard tree
she takes over my lap

and pressed between the pages
of milly molly mandy or dot and the kangaroo
i smell the aroma of four-leaf clover

said to be lucky
plucked near the broken gate

private

junior nurse quakes
her first male bed-bath
he's a lifetime smoker

his surgery days ago   rogue
cells in larynx – voice box
removed – can't speak

she shifts from one black
shoe to another   washer
in hand   mortified how to

tackle that private region
between his thighs
face aflame   *er – do they wash*

your arms and chest first?
he nods – she rinses the cloth
squares her shoulders

fixated on his manhood
shall i do your legs next?
he scrabbles for a notepad

grabs pencil stub   scribbles
shoves it in her face
you are doing it

they both laugh – for him
it's mute – the sponge is over
how could she

have been so foolish?

Snowy Mountains

We marvel at the wide horizon, a blue canopy arching from one
roll of hills to another, far on the other side. Cumulous clouds
play hide-and-seek with the sun, sketching transient images

of dragons and faces. Naked white trunks and bare limbs,
ache for leaves. Huge rocks clad in green moss, await
the snows of winter. Do they ski down magic slopes, dodging

sunset-coloured snow gums? We rattle over mountain streams
spotted with trout. Waterfalls cascade down rainbow-slicked rock faces.
Kangaroos stand in a circle, statues in conference. Nimbus clouds

growl and threaten, stretching damp tendrils towards the parched
earth, water running in all directions. Crows fly for shelter.
Wipers slosh away the rain, tarmac vanishing into the fog

of distant valleys. Lakes of the Snowy River scheme nestle
between eucalypts scented hills, in snatches of light, bright
as the returning sun. But listen! Do we hear songs and laughter

from those who built this wonder? Ghostly bulldozers roar, scrape and clank,
blades gouge earth, build roads, dams. Men tunnel through hills, concrete
sloshes, power stations crackle. Faces shimmer before me,

young and old. They shine in my mind like alpine wildflowers,
whispering of flight from war-torn Europe, of mountain laughter
and camaraderie, love and heartbreak, in Italian, Polish, French…

Orbs of Wonder

twin planets   fluffy surface
arrows of esse ready
to fly   delicate ephemeral

grown   not spun   soon to waft
on every breeze   dividing
multiplying   wanderers

refugees   seeking new
homes   mountain-top
meadow   some trapped

on roofs   others yet to journey
from pale green peduncles
for new lives   each tears loose

from their pincushion and sepals
rockets shoot forth   from launching pads
no cape Kennedy for these humble weeds

just hope

Icarus Moment

Analogous to Icarus in Bruegel's painting

spring glitter   far off surfers buzz
on boards   kids dream sandcastles
first swim of the season

pleased by my prowess –
then panic   can't touch bottom
no lifeguards to hear my cries

some sixth sense makes gordon stir
leaping from his towel   he strokes
to my side   gulls scream   billows banter

speeding us towards the beach a rip
carries us right back   every yard
gained quickly lost   frustration

midday glare   my boyfriend and i struggle
against the implacable sea   families frolic
surfers catch waves   us *invisible*   like Icarus

my best dog-paddle   strokes through
surging surf   we survive the tumult
of afternoon   my arms and legs scream

stop   Doris Day's voice rushes back
whatever will be will be…nineteen
and i'm ready to embrace the long sleep

i let my body sink   gordon shouts   *keep*
swimming   supreme effort   start again
the red disk drops away   i'm stroking

on automatic pilot   time loses
all meaning   i never imagined the sea
would be my tomb   twilight families

head home   i'm guessing we won't survive
much longer   wishful delusions   the beach
looks closer   second glance   shadowed figures

are larger…an incredible energy surge
speeds us ashore   i stagger sideways like a crab
wet sand dissolves   beneath my feet   i feel unbodied –

yet weighing a ton   disbelief   joy   *sweetie we've made it*
i collapse   sleeping the sleep of the utterly spent

Molly

little girl of four   molly
gives us strength to carry on –
should be the other way around

molly's lost her hair
but not her smile
there's this bug inside me

you see have to get rid of it
then my hair will grow
she dances for a little boy

he's sick too
did you vomit in school?
i did   *all over the floor*

pet scan   molly's tears
i get bored lying still
her mum says *soon be over pet*

i'll read you a story

mummy have another baby
if I'm not around
you'll have someone to love

mummy wipes her eyes   *guess what*
oh goody   *wherever I am*
I'll watch over my little sister

molly goes to hospital
pink case   barbie doll
fairy wings   a crown

operation's over   exultation
rogue cells dead   molly cradles
baby sister face aglow

she returns to school   shock relapse
molly smiles and slips away
holding their hands

The Three Sisters

in the chill morning air
three sisters stage an early parade
wrapped in fragrant gowns

of eucalypts and wildflowers
friends gaze at native shrubs
leaves quiver   twitter tweet

blue feather glimpse   legs like twigs
wrens hop from branch to branch
whipped cream piled high in a perfect sky

in the valley below fallen clouds
creep over creeks and tree ferns
embrace lichen-clad rocks

caress glass waterfalls   a gleam
of light   beams on red fungi
smiling   in fields of green moss

dewdrops flash rainbows
to mirror the escarpment
artists flaunt crayon and paintbrush

their paper and canvas images
framed

Mute

My heart breaks
when I see him
on the six o'clock news

No family left in Aleppo
just this boy of five   dragged
from his bomb-blasted home

Frozen   mute
hair and face powdered
with cement dust

Too young to know
he needs an ambulance
Robotically he touches

his damp forehead
stares blankly
at sticky red fingers

the sparkle stolen
from his young eyes

One Way

Most of us arrive in boxes
with flowers by the score
and no changes
of direction.

Friends lovers and family
glow with positive memories.
Gripes and grizzles unsaid –

not forgotten.

Some accept this date
with fate. Others hope
for a swift reprieve.

That day I pictured
the mirthless Reaper at the gate,
on the wait, for idiots like me
in shiny red cars.

Hand aloft, scythe by his side.
Stop!
        One way!
                Go back!

Clearing

bare to the waist
steadied by hobnailed boots
my father stands six-foot-six
dwarfed by the chosen eucalypt
in all its majesty

he plots the tangent of its fall
grips his axe   spits on calloused palms
a scarf cut   he grunts at every blow
the giant shakes   shudders
clutching the radiant sky

dad's muscles   slick with sweat
ripple on his back
the blade strikes deep
chips fly   i hear its last
despairing cry   fibres tear

boomp   clouds of dust
sweep through the bush
branches broken   scattered
leaves tremble   possums
flee in fright   ants

a moving mass of disaster
the naked trunk
stripped of bark
bleeds red   dad lifts

his sweat stained hat
wipes his brow
only a hundred acres to go

Pompom Parade

faces aglow   silver-haired couple
march along the timber way

white pompom doggie in tow
purple bow   paws in shades of

pink and blue   pram brigade dads
dawdle   gossip in the saline air

below   mums take sun-sparkle
breaks on sand   anglers' rods

oblique   white-capped waves

reel   squeal   and the wait
of seagulls dart and shriek
while pelicans   wings outspread

land   to check out the fun

Chainsaw Hero

river roars   brown water
surges   roof goes under
vehicle shudders against

a tree   i clamber high
in the branches   watching
my car plunge away

shivering   *i hear myself*
beg the tree to protect me
mulling over a lifetime

of lopping and chopping
minutes drag   a perpetuity
of fear   every muscle screams

my refuge sways
almost lose my grip
eight long hours   i'm praying

to a god i never knew
rain's back   almost dark
a helicopter swoops   last

rescue before night   it's then
i make my solemn vow
starting from now   i'll

never ever
lop another tree

Trophy

my husband rejoiced
at your sprightly dance
feathered treasure

clad in blue and grey
he forgot scans
and spots on the liver

for moments at a time

we watched for your sedate
mate   knowing you held
the genes of a vanished flock

you flew next door
to share your grace
and insouciance

an air rifle pellet stilled that
final frolic   your body a trophy
displayed in a girl's hands

the last blue wren
in our street

No Cause No Reason

a thief violated my safe clean home
leaving me angry   afraid   alone
ALS stole my speech   i can't scream

to the moon or curse the pitiless sun
i mouth the words   why me?
no drink or drugs   worked on the farm

my voice coaxed dogs from hidden
places   cut egocentric kids to size
railed against follies and television

thrilled to miracles and mountains
so many things to say and do
it's not me   tottering to the

loo   choking on mush   but then
then in the frosty sky of being
i begin to see   a new reality

why not me?

ALS: amyotrophic lateral sclerosis – a cruel progressive disease affecting cells in the brain and spinal cord

Farewell Visit

his son helps him
from the wheelchair
home from the hospice
morphine driver   maxalon

vomit bowl   he's gaunt and grey
and calls for the scissors
cutting up his driver's licence
and credit cards   one by one

asking his son *wheel me*
to the workshop
he caresses his lathe
and drill-press

the tool cabinet
built by hand
ready for retirement
he touches each in turn

saying *it's a shame*
a darned shame –
guess you'll all
be scattered to the winds

given only weeks
at most he begs his wife
help me end it all
she gulps   *darling*

you don't want me
going to gaol?
it'll happen soon
she shops   black skirt

size ten – usually
she's a fourteen
new blouse   neat collar
sews different buttons

his calm glance
your outfit for the funeral?
there's an ache in her throat
yes darling   i wanted

something special

Incan Idyll

Wrens chitter from rooftops and llama graze
with their *crias* on grass terraces above deep
ravines of the mind – and reality. Below, a silver
thread glitters, the upper Urubamba river.
It races to join the Amazon, headed for the sea.
Here, jagged peaks of vertiginous mountains
guard the ancient fortress of Machu Picchu.

Hidden hundreds of years, vines entwined,
walls broken by strangler figs and fallen
trees. Stones untrodden, panpipes silent –
the blood of conquest long dried
and washed away. This engineering
miracle almost forgotten –
until hacked from the jungle in
the twentieth century.

Safe in his noble citadel, Pachacuti,
the Inca king, shone in 18-carat gold and
feathered headdress, his fine garments
jewelled and embroidered with the same
precious metal. Imagine him gazing in wonder
at crystal water, gushing along channels,
cut into stone, with the sparkle in rainbows
of liturgical fountains, dancing between
the Temple of the Sun and his Royal Palace?

In his temple – crafted from quality stone
without mortar or steel tools – did he sing
hymns to the water god? Or worship
Viracocha, creator of the earth and heavens,
sun and moon, gods, humans – and all living things?
Did minions of the king pluck wildflowers
for his delight – purple heliotropium bells,
yellow senna and orange mirabilis?
Maybe he bit deep into aromatic flesh
of wild yellow passionfruit?

Doubtless, he enjoyed heroic tales
of his achievements. Walked on carpets
of red cantuta blossoms in sacred rituals.
Perhaps he played a bamboo flute.
Pachacuti wrote poems and stories.
And they say he may have prayed
his idyll would last forever…

Squirrel Maths

it's clear to me that every squirrel's tail
must be the envy of lesser creatures –
thick soft and held aloft   this furry
appendage hugging his lower body
an impressive backward curl at the top
while elm trees shiver and a chill breeze stirs
the last sere leaves   a squirrel – warm and cosy –
runs along a moss-encrusted wall   until a wide gap
in the bricks forces him to stop   he sits   meditates
flicks the hairs of his tail   eyeing the great divide
surely he'll never make it? should he take the risk?
long seconds pass   i see his calculations
are not lightly taken   he gathers every muscle
and takes a mighty leap   all grace and purpose

Psychiatry Ward

i

Antidepressants   exercise
And occupational therapy
Make the hours pass   but oh so slow

For some the headaches stop
And smiles push shadows and fears away
But the cloak of grey   hangs sodden

On those who stay ECT often
Starts their day in a world unchosen
Anxious   isolated by thoughts

That refuse to go away   tumbling
Like dirty washing   in a glass machine
Words too fast   too fast   or too slow

Psychiatrists   psychologists and sociologists
Research causes   try to cure effects
While patients search for themselves

In this abyss   they can't eat can't sleep
dreading   the horror of being awake…

ii

I must be somewhere in this chaos
Of words and explanations   Afraid
Of being seen   desperate   on being alone

I don't belong in this fog of muddled
Thoughts and lost hopes   least of all
Do I belong to myself

Blinding torments of despair
Make escape a beauteous thing
Longing to find   for just a moment

The joy of living others know

Massacre

the old man shivers
all that killing

so little choice
hard to reconcile now

keeps me awake at night
traps strychnine cyanide

warrens destroyed
gentle creatures   meant no

harm to anyone
if only they hadn't bred

in such multitudes
shaking his silver head

tremulous hands
drop into his lap

Incongruous

tang of chlorine
it's all shapes
and rare surprises

in the slow lane
of wrecks and relics
but one day eyes meet

and the music of laughter
ripples
down the pool

walkers   talkers   swimmers
united by a sense of the ridiculous
a woman wades by

with studied indifference
book held high to avoid splashes
as she reads

a confederacy of dunces

Celebration of Day

Old warrior's medals march as one
Pride and glory cheer their day
But mothers mourn vanished sons
And fresh-faced boys lie far away

Pride and glory cheer their day
Shadows of men march war's charade
And fresh-faced sons lie far away
Sticks and wheelchairs now parade

Shadows of men march war's charade
As losses grew our grief was tough
Sticks and wheelchairs now parade
They learnt to kill just out of school

Our losses grew   grief was tough
Red the poppies, red their blood
They learnt to kill just out of school
Fighting rats and lice and mud

Red the poppies, red their blood
God help our fathers, God help our sons
Fighting rats and lice and mud
Old warrior's medals march as one

Fox

you'll have to take me
from the tissue-lined box
by the seems of it

the fox fur
redolent of mothballs
blinked bright eyes
and draped itself

around the glitter
of her shoulders
ready to join

the Charleston dancers
beaded ladies
and black-tie partners

in patent shoes

Uluru Caper

morning coach revs   gallop of long legs and humps
caught in headlights   gulped by darkness   stars
shiver in the freezing air   the citron horizon
glows awake   knitted tree shapes   unstitched
on distant hills   the prehistoric monster

of *uluru* looms closer   dyed purple   then
blue colours switch   with the rising sun
we begin our climb   clawing upwards
plaques to the fallen and heart attacks
bring no comfort   leather gloves protect

from rough surfaces   the support
chain slides through my palms
on the first steep incline   i'm baffled how
japanese ladies   in high heels   manage
the ascent   in the chill morning breeze

we marvel at vistas reaching right
to *kata tjuta*   desert oaks   shrubs
and porcupine grass   in dull greens
cast shadows on the endless red plain
a taxing climb   when the chain ends

in blazing sun   i peel off layers   take a breath
and move on   enraptured by brilliant pink
succulent flowers – *parakeela* – others
rush on past   above we find mini valleys
long scars eroded in soft rock layers

reaching the cairn on top i gaze from azure
blue to the panorama way below   amazed
to find sparkling rock pools alive with shrimp
and fishes   how can they survive and thrive
in searing heat? when did they get there?
we attempt the return   trapped
in a mini ravine   without toe or
handholds   two red-faced
mammals on show   laughing   when

a chuckle of japanese proffer hands
i give a high five at emerging alive
saying *we've made it*   but he grins
don't speak too soon
still the descent to go

* Since this time, I have learnt it is offensive to Yankunytiavara and Pitjantjatjara people when anyone climbs Uluru, a sacred part of the Dreamtime. Now, showing respect for their culture, I would not do so.

Don't Call Me Madam

shady lane
discreet sign
massage
my shoulder pain cries
step inside

blinking   i see
skimpy-clad girls in a row
a hard-faced crone
man's the desk

i hesitate   then wait
beside dusty plastic flowers
she demands
i pay up front

a bloke ascends the stairs
behind long legs
skirt cut off at the bum
what to do?
i play dumb

a chatty lass relieves my knots
tight spots and hard muscle
blessed relief
but as i reach the door

male eyes leer my way
i'll have her

Prickle Bush

evil's torchlight knifes the shadows
effing bitch   where are ya?
you shiver in T-shirt and shorts

needled by a prickle bush   barely
breathing   wrists shackled at your back
longing to still your thumping heart

above the spinifex stars weep for pete
the smell of blood and death
shivers on the desert breeze

find the bitch   blackie
a dog's breath warms your face
thank god   he doesn't bark

another prisoner of chance?
cowed down by curses and blows?
van door slam   motor roar

you ache to run   red earth whispers
not yet   evil thuds back   *i'll have
ya soon bitch   rip ya gear off see how*

*hoity toity ya are then…*voice fading
he whistles the dog   the van revs
twin red taillights disappear

he's gone – or ready to pounce?
you wait an hour   maybe three
darkness   houdini moment

zigzag   bumping into ant towers
stuart highway   road train   brakes
screech   you a scarecrow   blinded

by searing lights   ripped shorts
scratched legs   bloodied wrists
waving above your head

help…help me find pete…
evil has a gun

Naked

cliffs and rolling hillocks
overlook the tumbling surf
footprints track salutations
on the beach brown bodies
and faces worship the sun
we fling off tops   shorts   sandals…

false skins of the world   our
feet slipping and squeaking
as we run   wavelets splash   sucking
sand under bare feet   lacy froth
swirls   gifting yellow green
sea grass   neptune's necklace

and shells   a dark blue line cuts
sea from sky   wisps of blake white
cirrus clouds brushstroked above
the spindrift teases hair and face
caressing   each bare torso as one
with the saline tang   unencumbered

by the prudery of clothing   it awakens
a primal need to cavort in the deep
translucent green water rising
into great liquid walls   hesitating
at that moment of transcendence
preceding the drop   folding   falling

and thundering towards
the furrowed shore   boiling
with undertones of treasure
swept   swirled and foaming
into exhilaration

Parched

starlings drifting like clouds of smoke from
campfires of long ago   whirling   swooping

mingling   soaring   above stark shapes of naked
trees   sun-dried fish pattern   the lost water hole

cracked   and broken mud tiles the river bed
sere bullock   twisted death throes   parched leather

atop piled brown leaves   ghostly black men driven
to a precipice   *quamby quamby*   *save me save me*

can we forgive our ancestors
       the terror of terra nullius?

Nazca Lines

single-engine plane
weigh your options
balance the load
someone asks   *where's colleen?*

i joke *too heavy   on the other plane*
they laugh at the thought
of our tiny friend
banished from this flight

our plane swoops and dives
in the morning light
above barren hillsides
wings point to the nazca lines

geoglyph carvings made long ago
some large as a 747
outlined by stones
cameras click and snap

our pilot zooms closer
for the best shots
condor   monkey   spider   spaceman
moments for reflection

on nazca folk of long ago
making ceramics   textiles
and digging underground aqueducts
that still function

Perfection

the perfect novel   a distant atoll
glimpsed from the sharp-shingled shore
of striving   wavelets of hope foam

and groan around my toes sinking
under my feet   *tries hard*   screeches a
seagull   *but does not always succeed*

very good   mutters a crab walking sideways
at some things   I breathe the briny music of air
and sea   is this is the way it's meant to be?

nothing can replace the joy of creation
in this quest   and yes i've done my best

Time for Lunch

my grandson   aged ten
offers to make fresh pasta
i glance at the clock
one p.m.   i'm hungry –
it's too late
oh gran please   please

he puts on an apron
cleans the bench
measures flour   makes a well for eggs
mixes wet with dry
punches and pounds
chants   *fold and push   fold and push*

smooths it into a ball
hold out your hands gran
he puts it through the machine
i support unfolding pastry   famished –
surely it's thin enough?
he laughs   *not yet*   tightens a screw

through again   three times
it's thinner   longer
and almost transparent
he boils ribbons of fettuccine
four minutes   i drool at the aroma –
garlic   chopped tomato and basil
sprinkled with parmesan

three o'clock
i'm weak with hunger –
time to dine

Master Two

blonde cupcake of
joy and new sensations
the boy tunes his body

instrument of life   he
dances   twists   turns
shrugs   watches a bug

starlit smiles   shy glances
don't stray behind the counter
or you'll be iced

Paradox

red leaves stroke each other
whispering of life and death
don't be afraid   facing the end

is profoundly liberating   you'll
confront mortality in your own way
an inner journey of awareness

and acceptance   reflect on
important things   abandon
the trivial   give your life

meaning   ditch show and differences
find a passion   cherish each moment
surrender to being   heal relationships

for inner peace and joy   hating
takes too much energy
abandon things beyond repair

each red   gold or yellow leaf
drifts down   falling   spinning
dreaming   for eternity

Mellow Sunday

parents recline on rugs
scent of mown grass
mellow jazz quartet

picnic baskets   strawberries
ice cream cones crunch
glasses clink   sav blanc

grandpa snores
grey curls   shiny pate
he soaks the morning sun

blonde kids dance
pink babies gurgle
lovers hold hands

and a black man   strong arms
vivid yellow shorts   matching sneakers
strolls among the anglo beige

exotic leopard   in a field of sheep

Pisco Sour

i

our luxury hotel hidden by a wall
offers citron   coriander and vanilla cream
to pamper plump bodies

we cuddle soft towels   watch twin TV
luxuriate in king-size beds   enjoy
de luxe showers   pacific breezes

caress us   umbrellas chatting
above white sun chairs   waiters
bring the clink of piña coladas

and cocktails to the pool
with strawberries
and tiny pink parasols

ii

pisco sour   ailing peruvian
landscape   it never rains
no shining path

beside the dusty road
shanty towns derelict
piles of sand   rubble

grove of trees   planted
to stop the dispossessed
building makeshift homes

the barefoot poor
brave searing heat
awaiting the water cart –

if they can pay

Cambridge Man

i

urbane and debonair
ironic smile   rapier eyes
every whisker trimmed
raconteur   musician
lover of balzac   ts eliot
long walks   french wine
and summer parties for fifty
in his garden

ii

steps slow and faltering
almost blind   deaf
hair awry   unkempt beard
twisted spine   nerveless fingers
scuffed shoes   missing pockets
awkward buttons
and lost rooms

ravages
          of
                  time

Paean

nine in the morning
blaze of sun   garden shrivel
i can't wait for sprinkler fun

birds-nest ferns rejoice
when drops of moisture
ski down sloped leaves

to heart and roots
rainbows of liquid
tantalise

magpie eyes size up the risk
desperate for a shower   throat
dry   she darts   flies   perches

out of reach   head on one side
watching the hand that holds
the hose   it moves closer

her sudden swoop   under
the downpour   magpie
raises one wing   lifts

the other   soaked from
feather to skin   jewelled
by diamonds   she preens

in a wattle tree   lifts her beak
a black and white paean
to rain

Cairns Rendezvous

mist creeps from the lush
mountains to caress the city
moisture drips from palm

trees   taxis rare as pearls
in smoked oysters   optimistic
passengers   go nowhere fast

but at last   a cab to the centre
of town   fast food outlet   despair
of limp salads and greasy fries

colonial-style café   an embrace
of lattice colonnades   soft
lighting and ceiling fans

purring like giant cats
dark-eyed waiter bears
crisp greens   chicken

and grainy bread   fresh fruit salad
zings with melon   strawberries
snuggle into cream   and i savour grapes

plump as midnight kisses

Indian Hawker

silver beard   powder-blue turban
campfire tang   stories whirling like smoke
from far off lands   dervishes   temples   saris

local lad seated at his feet gazes in wonder
aromatic johnny cakes somersault in a pan
white horse munches hay   wagon drawers red

green   yellow   promise a thousand delights
the hawker spies a customer   *dress missus*?   she shakes
her head   *too cheap*   his smile of guile   large white teeth

i've plenty more   the dress moves to the upper
drawer   while he holds a glittering necklace
against her scrawny throat   *for you missus*

special price beguiled   she sniffs   cheap scents
velvet bows   nestle in wispy hair   *a woman of
discrimination*   *like you*   *wants only the best*

here's a dress more to your taste   he reaches
inside the top drawer   *feel the quality of this one*
work-worn hands caress the thin fabric

how much?   he names a figure   twice the
original price   she extracts the sum with élan
scurries away   laden with treasures

and that   thought the boy   *is how it's done*

Gallipoli

shattered femur   splintered skull
rusting water flask   twisted barrel of a gun
lost   among the grass
flame of poppies   weeping

boys of long ago   brutalised into men
the sea turned red   as comrades fell
others struggled on   surviving
this hell of jagged cliffs

shots   cries   explosions
aussie fought turk
in this vale of sorrow
at shrapnel valley
they all died
us   and them

and in the gooseflesh ice of silence
their voices scream as one

WHY?

Sacred Moments

i

dying is a sacred moment   i lost
the fear of death the day he
died   the whole room lit up

when his spirit left the physical husk
of his body   uniting with souls in other
dimensions of reality

i've seen ghostly apparitions
physical manifestations of his survival
intuition   ESP   and all sorts of psychic

phenomena defy explanation
sadness keeps his memory alive
i'm not angry – it makes you old

ii

birth brings the same stillness
and expectation – when my grandson arrived
i lost the fear of life   our daughter isn't

blood-related   she's kin of the soul
i'm lucky to have grandchildren
their vibrant joy enriches my days

Bachelors' Buttons

florrie's son waves them away
have fun girls   says joe   *be back*
by four   *chill evening mists drift*
in these parts   she grins   *you'd think*

i was a kid   *not your mother*
under luminous afternoon skies
florrie strolls with cousin joy   they
gather buttercups and bachelors'

buttons   radiant with light   florrie
enhances her posy with red gum tips
hands cup crystal water from the creek
dripping through her fingers

scent of wild mint and wattle
lyrebird shimmy   tail feathers
tremble   in gran's delight she
forgets the creep of night   fog

clouds trees   stones   paths
joy turns and turns again   *gran*
do you know the way back?
florrie shivers   *thought i did…*

she fears there's nothing
to be done   her son could never find
them in this murk   a sudden boom
echoes in the gloom   florrie's feet

and heart dance   *it's joe –*
signalling our way home
damp and weary they climb
the steep incline   scratched

by wait-a-while vine and bramble
they clamber over rocks   clutching
at tussocks   joe's booming
river of sound leads them on

two bedraggled figures emerge
from the fog   joe drops the mallet
near the hollow log – his drum –
two strides and he's at florrie's side

she beams – her wildflower
posy frayed but intact

Caijon Del Maipo

i

veiled sun   snarl of traffic   we choke
in the taste and smell   our guide
drives us far from city smog
far from stray dogs on mats

outside shops   far from graffiti
which defiles ancient statues
in the *maipu* canyon we breathe
fresh air perfumed by wildflowers

horses graze on swamps near
mineral-rich stream and glass
waterfalls leap from peaks
of the snowy andes

ii

we lunch at Casa Bosque – this fairy-tale
house of wood speeds us from reality to
fantasy   cypress trunks   limbs and roots
stripped of bark   smooth as a baby's cheek

inform this marvel of architectural creation
one flowing organic structure leads to another
an undulating roof   in contrast to the blue
chili sky   dances with fountains   inside

rainbows of colour shine from alcoves
with stained glass   the winding staircase leads
to a sapling balcony for brides   their veiled
images reflected in mirrors edged with carved timber

a hint of incense emanates from niches for saints
and outsize insects spill light on lively murals
above flickering candelabra   timber beams
make a straight statement or circle   solid doors

boast old iron hinges   and a touch
of stonework contrasts with mellow
yellow adobe walls hiding eight
thousand tyres   we imagine

countless hours spent
by craftsmen transforming this
vision into a prize-winning work of art –
all this and superb food too

Rains of Change

we walk pavements slicked
with rains of change
the old year wallows
in its last days

tinsel trickles down from trees
a black dog lurks with a beggar
in a shop doorway
illuminated by commerce

*help me I'm homeless
spare a coin*…it's good to see
things have improved
in post-Brexit Britain

Perfect Evening

in a fragrant corner of her garden
breathing in the scent of lilacs
she dreamed of a perfect evening

how grand it was to stand with him
fallen leaves spinning in rings
until the moon fled behind

dark clouds   shivering
at the plangent howl of dingoes

when he drawled   *it's forgotten
how to rain*   and took his leave
shattered shards cut like glass

Eternal Land

Craggy peaks gaze into deep canyons
with solidified ripples of rocks
millions of years old.

And mesa, residue of
mountains, cling to their past.
Rain, wind and time, wander

across vast plateaus
and rocks like some lost city
lie abandoned in the great heat

Certain formations lie like serpents
curled up among the spikes of spinifex
The ultera plant, native to this eternal land

oozes whitish sap, protecting from sunburn.
And oases of Cycads dream back
to rainforests and dinosaur days.

Boneyard

it's a shame   a shame
five hundred men denied a name
under the white man's road

tourists come   but never see
shadow ancestors   who cry to me
black men   harsh bright sun

time when tribe and land were one
exiled men   troubled eyes
chained   maimed   brutalised

unrespected   unsuspected
under the white man's road
south wind sigh   roar of sea

throw sand
spirits free

Breathless

skeletal   gasping
eye whites yellow

morphine for pain
i try my cardboard coffin
decorated with flowers
and angels   i'm ready

for that eternal moment
each day enriched
by company

i make people laugh
a hug or shared glance
warms my heart

laboured breath
i gasp *come sit by me*
she holds my hand

i float in some mysterious space
between this world and the next
waiting   the eternal silence

Emotions

where do you put anger
that keeps you awake at night?
load it onto on a barge
float it away into the sunset
barge after barge low in the
water   until the burning tornado
is spent and you sleep

where do you carry your
happiness? let it it pulse in your
hear   sing with the lark
drift on the wind and in
the soughing pines
dancing in the eyes
of a lover

where do you hide your
sorrow? let it linger in the perfume of
dried roses   crackle in yellowing letters
whisper from the leaves of trees
ache in snatches of old songs
return in memories –
and drive the pain of poems

Greetings

Happy Christmas Ellen writes, our
kids all turning fifty – how can it be?
I only feel that age myself but
as my father said on his death bed
there's not much in it

Told Sue of my grandkids – flute, guitar,
youth orchestra, off to play in the south
of France. She wrote, *Fancy yours being
so clever: must be in the genes.* One of hers
is back from a year's exchange in Paris. She
has eight grandchildren, even a few great grandkids.

Joyous New year! Resolutions to keep:
curb my anger, banish envy, smile at
those who recall things which never
happened, yet forget what took place
last week. Be less judgemental.
And always find something good
to say – a comment on hair or
dress can make your day.

Peace on Earth, says another card,
Annie asking, *what makes intelligent
humans blow each other to pieces*?
Another day, another target. Let love
unite creeds, cultures, religions.
Hugs all around, weep with strangers,
breathe the heady scent, a thousand
flowers, concrete bedded with blossoms

One card from another friend: *Shaky as an old fence. Not even
a stray cat drops by for a meal. Ready to go but the
lord won't take me, Hope you get all the things your
heart desires…* Fendi handbags? Italian shoes?
At our age it's titanium hips, heart valves, hearing
aids, shunts, a tuck here, lift there, dye the hair.

Perrie writes, *there's an aura in old houses…*
Each room knows scenes of tragedy and
happiness. Used to feel my husband's spirit
still around. Now there's only silence. The
teaching bureaucracy is driving my daughter
crazy. Data drives and tick the boxes.
Little time left for kids

No card from Elissa. Calm as the moon,
she's waiting. Pain controlled by morphine.
Cocooned within her family. Hasn't stopped
her forty a day addiction. What's it matter now?
Friends visit her twice weekly,
sharing tales of our Belfield days.
Over thirty years nursing the old
demented and frail. Couldn't have
known a better friend

Hadn't seen the next lady for a while.
Missed her cheerful chats, butterfly stickers
and hand-written missives. Rang, leaving a message.
She tapped out a letter on her grumpy antique typewriter.
Scrappy piece of paper, aflame with indignation. *Did you
expect me to wait on the telephone for three
years until you called? Never want see or hear from
you ever again. Couldn't care less about your novel.*
Silly duck. Dare I suggest she could have called me?

Fig Tart and Tea

hot in here   a bit better
than outside   fan yourself
with the menu
                    words imbed edges

into our ears *girl   wake up to yourself*
we've got to talk – mum i'm eighteen can do what i like
i don't think so – nobody can

we eavesdrop on this tango
of incomprehension
           sip flat white   nibble fig tart

It's all about time management
don't want to hear this –
while we're paying your way –

sentences smoulder   break into pieces
nouns huddle in the turgid air
verbs jump with outrage   coffee-scented

bomp bomp bomp music
words on the run from reason

cacophony of ire

Earthquake

Thought it was an earthquake
but it was me…

Waves thunder, gulls scream
crushing pain in my chest
I gasp for breath, left arm tingles

Where are those bloody pills?
Sweat drips from my brow
I'd call an ambulance

but forgot my mobile
Ticker leaps and flutters
against my ribs.

A surfer ambles past
Kids laugh, motorbike roar
My words falter, on the cusp

of being spoken
Lost, on broken beach walls

Dad

in the pub
dad drank away exhaustion
recited dangerous dan macgrew
accepted jobs
shook calloused hands

on agreements
mateship the glue
that laughed him through
days when life was all too hard
he slaked a thirst

grown large
in the killing fields
of poison and traps
in rural new south wales
and graziers gloated
       over pest-free paddocks

wool clips
like a lottery win
every year

but in old age dad
felt haunted
by all the bunnies killed

for survival

Epiphany

Whoosh of wings, flash of red and blue
Twisting vines, hairy tree-ferns, purple fungi
and rotting logs, a renaissance of moss.

Eucalypts, turpentine and sassafras,
a fragrance of wild mint, herbs and violets –
water gurgling over rocks

Willy-wagtails dancing, in the golden light
Shining leaves atremble, in the tree tops
And with a sudden hush, one fluffy cloud

is weeping, glittering raindrops.
Translucent orbs of wonder, magnified
by light, drifting slowly, one by one,

rainbows in flight.

A Grief Ago

Tender, hand-held moment
The light of love raw in his eyes
A toast to you, my darling
Haven't had such fun
in ages

I cling to him
staring down his prognosis
Four months – sixteen weeks
How can it be?

Ella

ella
grabs
two chairs
cardboard box
teddies dollies a monster
train car boat or plane?

chuff roar whistle wobble
balance soar puff giggle
swim ski dance and juggle
splash crash laugh and wriggle

no sand in the bucket
stars in her eyes

Abu Dhabi

fishing village singing
sand dunes   bedouin
and tents below the glow

of stars and a crescent moon
fast forward forty years   mountains
of glass   there's no mystery in this history

fuelled by oil   one tower block competes
with another   solid palaces replaced
by seven-star hotels   one

with quarter-million-dollar suites
plated in gold   no taxes to pay
and   they say   enough crude

to last over a hundred years
while guest workers   sick and spent
are flown back home   in this city built

on shifting sands of global warming
and climate change

Gone

He's gone
she strokes his silver hair
my first love

kisses his forehead
turns back the linen
caresses his cold feet

blotched and turning blue
dearest one it's been fifty years
never anyone else

now I'm all alone
her wail shivers to the ceiling
and curls around the room

Hovercraft XPT

shadowed by that long night
the express rocks and shimmies
leaving a twin　　silver wake
glittering in moonlight

passengers play cards　　read
and thumb screens – i sleep
in dreams my hovercraft XPT
whizzes me through valleys

and above shivering reeds
speeding across a lake
water splashes into my face
but in the race for Sydney

sudden announcement
blinks　　sleepers awake
startled to find ourselves
stranded – a broken rail

an hour late already
arrival time unclear
text messages ping
into changed plans

at last the carriages
pick up their stitches
our garment of travel
wobbles　　chattering

delight at farms orchards
hills and dew-wet morning
fields drenched in gold –
a sight better than darkness

Goodbye

for Gordon

I don't want to leave you
and all the earthly things
which I hold dear

My TV, video, stereo world
of Reeboks and deals,
long lunches and film launches

Battles to be fought – and won
Tissue-wrapped projects to be done
My shiny red lambswool soft car

and smoky model trains,
on silver tracks Our tree safe
flower-scented garden,

of bird twitter and dreams
Cats with enigmatic eyes
Moon glow star still nights,

and sun-drenched mornings
Rain trembling on new leaves
Shy blossoms that breeze in spring

Heart-stop glances, marriages,
and graduations. Birthday cake
champagne bubble celebrations

Cheek kissed, smiling tomorrows,
and journeys to exotic places. Shadowed
faces of my grandchildren, yet unborn

How can I say goodbye
while loved ones dance on
to the music of life?

Frozen Time

you shiver
and know not why
then glimpse her shadowy form

cloaked in gown and hood
seen   unseen   rustle of silk
she descends a demolished

staircase   steps through a sandstone
wall into the archives   shrouded
in mystery and dust motes

mullion window   shaft of light
she bends over parchment letters
book   quill   enigmatic smile

white hands tremble
jewels scintillate
icy blast of frozen time

Greek Tragedy

in a shaft of breakfast sunlight
it's a Herculean task
to heft my load
the rope is strong

i zip to the top
my prize within reach
but it slips
down

i pull it up
down
up   pale yellow
pliable

ready to transform
down
damn
like Sisyphus i struggle on

watching
soon i'll roll this precious load
into shelter   my new home
a dozen or more tries

eureka
my eight legs quiver
the leaf plummets to earth

Hatzolah

wave glitter   salt tang
on this glorious day
a guy jumped
landing on rocks
far below

emergency help abseils down the cliff
hatzolah first on the scene
the patient moans   face ashen
breath ragged   he whispers
tell my wife and kids
i'm sorry

the hatzolah man says *you'll be okay, mate*
help is on the way   sombre at the multiple fractures
heartsick   they always express regrets

awaiting the police launch
he holds the patient in his arms

above seagulls gyre and cry
the patient's breath labours stops
the medic closes his eyes

a prayer ebbs and flows
with the slosh of waves
and a plane flies on by

Hatzolah: a Jewish organisation that addresses emergency situations in collaboration with paramedics

Slippery Trout

it slides through fingers   trembles
on cautious lips   often not what
it seems   emerges in fragments
garnered over time

changes for convenience   or gain
half of it   torments and damages
repute   the whole can set
you free   people crave

the substance   for history
memory of it   wriggles risky
waterways   folk die for it
complicated   easy to miss

the river of dreams   makes
symbols of it   the first casualty
of conflict   some people carry
it lightly   often invisible

or mistrusted   it swims with us
throughout life   risks death with
the holder   unless we write it
down   sought in courts of law

sworn on bibles
truth

Last Trip to Manly

for Gordon

Sydney Harbour Bridge slips away
Wan sun, dark clouds, wavelets tremble
My husband's face looks grey
The Opera House sails past.
Botanical Gardens – spring blossoms heavy
with foreboding

Tourists chatter. Pinchgut reality
Gordon sighs, a grin. *As a boy*
it was my joy to ride the ferry
I loved the roil of storms
back and forth to Manly

Wind and water caressed my face…

When it docked, I hid in the toilets.
Until the return journey.

I'm a house clinging to cliffs
A wife – my heart spills pink flesh
and black seeds, lost in the wake
Four months. Sixteen weeks – how can it be?
Thrum of motors, back thrust
Midday glitter

With hospitals and prognosis far away
we step ashore. And I hear him say
Hang the diet. Let's enjoy this lovely day
Sweet salmon, crunch of salad
Sip dry white…

Tender, hand-held moment
A toast to you, my darling

haven't had such fun
in ages

Waiting for a Train

Young man sways. Loud hello, stink of booze.
He slumps onto the seat, touches her arm,
swigs from a bottle, wrapped in brown paper.

She chats to keep him calm. *He asks, are you
a teacher? You know so much.* She laughs, *I'm a nurse
Doctors couldn't do major operations without us*

He nods. Same for me – *brickies' labourer.
We're essential. I like nurses. They often save me life
after an overdose. Wake, needle in me arm.*

Me mother's from Qatar. Father Malaysian
He stares. *You're so white.* She laughs. *Actually,
it's a mutation. They say the default colour is black*

He says, *You're right – we all came from Africa.
I read a lot – do you?* She nods. *Among my favourite
pastimes.* He offers the bottle. *I've got hepatitis. Like*

a drink? She shakes her head. *Alcohol is bad
for the liver. Why not stop drinking?* He looks sad.
I can't. Hate myself. She pats his shoulder.

He swallows. *No worries luv –
I'll soon get back on track.*

Malingering

marge breathless on the stair
hubby says *walk   fresh air*
can't believe his wife's so lazy

'course you'll have a thumping
head if you don't get out of bed
eat decent meals   moans   vomits

just to annoy me   barely drinks doc says
she has the flu   by Sunday she'll be

fine   I keep telling her to get up
come and watch TV with my sister
and me   but she just lies there

whispers no just go – women!
can't abide malingering   the
program over   I bid sis goodnight

marge want a drink?
just say yes or no
marge…

Mall Dreaming

you've been dreaming of bras and things
floating in free space   one with fancy cups
and a rose to seduce   it's not enough for you
to take paper scissors and create dirty chic

an eternity of witching   for his eyes only
even kids on the pavement will cotton on
to what's taking place in the pumpkin
patch of life   take this eclipse of meaning

wearing just jeans   check the time on your
swarovski   say gee up to your pony   a
valley girl like you has nowhere to hide
secrecy used as a weapon or a veil   sky part

of the sea   paddling among stars   touch her
and she flashes bluish light that dissipates
as if she's dissolved   among the never seen

and eternity   glimpsed in fashion

Sacred Rites

a disciple clad in white – veil-long sleeves –
grandpa selects a hive puffs his smoker
bee buzz calms   tingling excitement   his
hand dives   grabs a frame of wax oozing
honey but it isn't funny when he stumbles

and takes a tumble   not even the yellow
scent – honeysuckle azalea – brings the old
chap awake   the doctor shakes his grizzled
head   closes grandpa's eyes   *heart attack
no breath or pulse* his widow wails and sighs

*but doctor   he can't be dead – who'll
attend his hives?* the undertaker shuts
the shiny lid and drives grandpa's
cosy casket away   friends and family
gather   sharing tears and laughter

recall grandpa's loving ways   things
to ponder and warm their days
in the scent of lily and incense   the room
reels black with loss   his veiled widow
blots her swollen eyes   *i know*

*there's nothing to bring him back
but ease my sorrow a little please –
retrieve the family necklace
the one he's wearing   with a crest
of bees* the undertaker lifts the lid

before he can collect the prize
hairs on his neck begin to rise   slight
movement   the expired chest –
the doctor can't believe his eyes
faint breath   weak pulse   it's called

suspended animation – a first for me – the
widow wife swoons and hits the floor –
the doctor cries   *move aside   give her air*
grabs his phone   *operator it's urgent –
two for the ambulance…*

Sardonic

one-eyed stone   twisted sardonic grin
sits watching us at the station
i've never seen it there before

its sudden appearance has me
spooked   surely it's not an ASIO spy
sent to surveil commuters?

clever disguise   posing as a rock
does it wonder what i'm writing?
and snap me on hidden cameras?

do microphones record and scrutinise
my every word? don't look now
but i vow to keep my mouth shut

except to say no stones were hurt
in the creation of this poem

Athens Train

three young musicians linger
beside me   cacophony of strident
notes   missed keys long and loud

then a squabble shouts
into life   just behind a youth sits
near me   hand trembling   cobra ready

to strike   distraction their game
robbed earlier   paris metro
before he can grab my wallet

i hug my bag   showing the
pickpocket my back   afraid other
passengers are in the gang

journey's end   i rush through
loitering station cave   heavy with
the stink of old urine   and young poverty

needled with despair

Gather

Ramble in the tropical forests of poetry
gather words and phrases   locutions
meet and elbow others aside

wanting to escape   strangler figs
and twining vines have no other
ambition but to save themselves

annihilation always a risk

idioms swing in dizzy circles
above my head   some useless
for my task others don't dare

to ask   nonce words wail and cry
me me me   they may deserve
a place in the poem   rich

with new meanings   others wear the faded
cloaks of cliché   waiting to be reborn
one demands the history of baboons

and monkeys while a poet
pecks his path through shoals
of chances with keyboard or pen

Rescue

dad sits in the warm glow,
lost in red and yellow images

flames lick   caress   and consume
in this lust of lively life,

blazing tongues leap,
coals start   snap   and crackle

he dreams a story of life
intermingled with destruction

red sparks explode and soar
do they join other stars

in the firmament? Below
a glimpse of frantic sugar ants

rushing this way and that
desperate to escape

his calloused hands
position a timber bridge

above the inferno   they
rush to scramble aboard

dad carries them outside
into the moonlit night –

seconds from being roasted

Dazzle

He walks the cracked pavement of life
gathering motifs and figures of speech
words meet and elbow other words aside

keen to dazzle the street they swing
in dizzy circles inside his head   some
are useless for his task   others

hesitate to ask for inclusion
certain egos shout *me me me* though
they deserve no place in the piece

a few shimmer with new meanings
others wear shabby cloaks of cliché
waiting to be reborn   others doubt

the ontological concepts of the piece
and the poet picks up tropes with his stick

Fallen Star

she rises with the sun   red wavelets shush
rush of criss-cross currents riffle the surface
she wades pools edged with moss

watches bridal veils and spindrift tails
touches linen-fold sandstone
liquid lace foams around her feet

while pelicans soar   above the roiling surf
she treads shoals of khaki kelp   pink coral
and neptune's necklace adorns a mermaid's

throat   sea shells   her conchology delight
fish gasp and gulp   abandoned by the tide
she bends to their rescue

and finds   a fallen star

www.ingramcontent.com/pod-product-compliance
Lightning Source LLC
Chambersburg PA
CBHW070917080526
44589CB00013B/1330